AF228856

# Tarsiers

Julie Murray

**abdopublishing.com**

Published by Abdo Kids, a division of ABDO, PO Box 398166, Minneapolis, Minnesota 55439.
Copyright © 2018 by Abdo Consulting Group, Inc. International copyrights reserved in all countries.
No part of this book may be reproduced in any form without written permission from the publisher.

Printed in the United States of America, North Mankato, Minnesota.

102017

012018

Photo Credits: Alamy, iStock, Minden Pictures, National Geographic Creative, Shutterstock

Production Contributors: Teddy Borth, Jennie Forsberg, Grace Hansen

Design Contributors: Christina Doffing, Candice Keimig, Dorothy Toth

Publisher's Cataloging-in-Publication Data

Names: Murray, Julie, author.

Title: Tarsiers / by Julie Murray.

Description: Minneapolis, Minnesota : Abdo Kids, 2018. | Series: Nocturnal animals |
           Includes glossary, index and online resource (page 24).

Identifiers: LCCN 2017908180 | ISBN 9781532104084 (lib.bdg.) | ISBN 9781532105203 (ebook) |
           ISBN 9781532105760 (Read-to-me ebook)

Subjects: LCSH: Tarsiers--Juvenile literature. | Nocturnal animals--Juvenile literature. |
           Animals--Apes & Monkeys, etc--Juvenile literature.

Classification: DDC 599.8--dc23

LC record available at https://lccn.loc.gov/2017908180

# Table of Contents

# Tarsiers

Tarsiers live in Southeast Asia.

They are found in trees.

5

They have soft **fur**. Many are brown or gray.

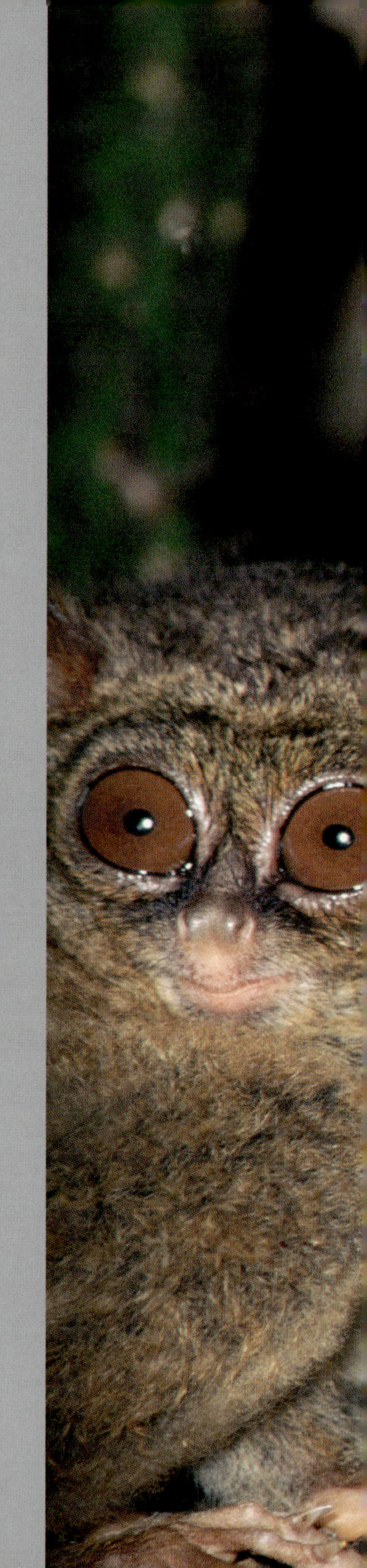

They have long tails. They use them to **balance**.

9

Tarsiers are very small. But they are good hunters.

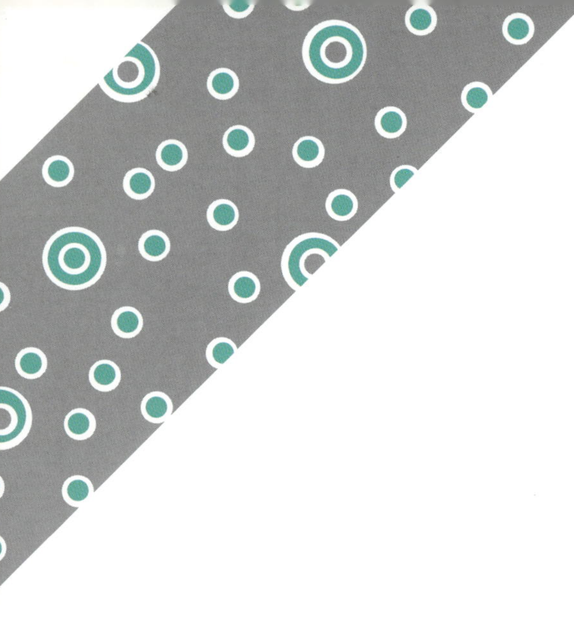

They sit in the dark.

They wait for **prey**.

Their eyes are big. This helps them see well at night.

They have long fingers.
They use them to hold
onto trees and food.

17

They have long back legs.
They can jump far. They
leap to catch their food!

They eat insects. They also eat frogs.

# Features of Tarsiers

large eyes

long back legs

long fingers and toes

long tail

# Glossary

**balance**
stay upright and steady.

**fur**
the short, fine, soft hair of some animals.

**prey**
an animal that is hunted for food.

# Index

Asia 4

color 6

eyes 14

fingers 16

food 12, 16, 18, 20

fur 6

legs 18

size 10

tail 8

Visit **abdokids.com** and use this code to access crafts, games, videos, and more!

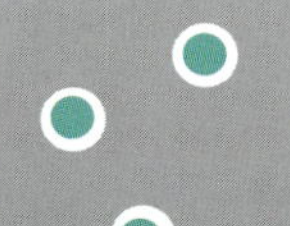

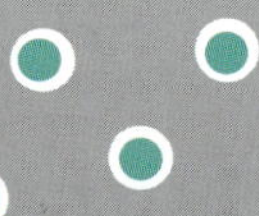